CRaZY NaTuRe™

Animal Mimics

Marie Racanelli

PowerKiDS
press.

New York

To Milo

Published in 2010 by The Rosen Publishing Group, Inc.
29 East 21st Street, New York, NY 10010

First Edition

Editor: Joanne Randolph
Book Design: Greg Tucker
Photo Researcher: Jessica Gerweck

Photo Credits: Cover © Photoshot/age fotostock; p. 5 Darlyne A. Murawski/Getty Images; p. 7 Ben Hall/Getty Images; pp. 9, 13 Shutterstock.com; p. 9 (inset) John Cancalosi/Peter Arnold, Inc.; p. 11 Altrendo Nature/Getty Images; pp. 14–15 © Superstock/age fotostock; p. 17 © Viola's Photo Visions Inc./ Animals Animals; p. 19 Jeff Foott/Getty Images; p. 21 George Grail/Getty Images.

Library of Congress Cataloging-in-Publication Data

Racanelli, Marie.
 Animal mimics / Marie Racanelli. — 1st ed.
     p. cm. — (Crazy nature)
 Includes index.
 ISBN 978-1-4358-9382-5 (library binding) — ISBN 978-1-4358-9856-1 (pbk.) — ISBN 978-1-4358-9857-8 (6-pack)
 1. Mimicry (Biology)—Juvenile literature. I. Title.
 QH546.R33 2010
 591.47'3—dc22
                                        2009034093

Manufactured in the United States of America

CPSIA Compliance Information: Batch #WW10PK: For Further Information contact Rosen Publishing, New York, New York at 1-800-237-9932

Contents

What Is Mimicry?

There are thousands of animals in our world. Some of these animals are **predators**, and some of them will end up as **prey**. They all need to eat. They all need to keep themselves safe. Some animals, over time, have **adapted** certain features that match those of other **species**. These features fool their predators and help the animals live longer. These animals are called **mimics**.

Mimics copy the appearance, action, or sound of another animal that predators fear or do not like to eat. The animals they copy are called models. Let's learn more about these copycats in nature.

The caterpillar of the spicebush swallowtail butterfly looks like a snake or lizard because of the shape of its back end and the eyespots.

Copycat!

There are different kinds of mimicry. One kind is called Batesian mimicry. It is named after Henry Walter Bates, a naturalist. He discovered that some weaker animals adapted to their **environment** by copying or looking like **dangerous** animals. These weaker animals often have no **defenses**, such as stingers or **poisons**. Instead, they look very much like other animals that do, and so their enemies leave them alone.

One example of Batesian mimicry is the hoverfly. Over time this fly has adapted to have yellow and black stripes like a bee. Animals know that a bee will sting them, so they leave this kind of fly alone.

The hoverfly, or flower fly, not only looks like a bee or wasp, but it also drinks nectar, as bees do. These flies cannot sting, as bees do, though.

A Closer Look at Batesian Mimicry

Coral, king, and milk snakes are excellent examples of Batesian mimicry. Coral snakes are poisonous. King and milk snakes are not. Coral snakes have colorful **scales** in bands of black, red, and yellow. The yellow bands always touch the red ones. These colors announce the snakes' deadly poison. Some king and milk snakes also have bands of red, black, and yellow, but they are arranged in a different order.

It is not always easy to tell these snakes apart. A predator will often leave king or milk snakes alone because it sees their colors and believes that they are poisonous, too.

This king snake has adapted its coloring as a defense. Predators see bands like those of the coral snake (inset) and leave the snake alone.

Eat at Your Own Risk!

Another type of mimicry is called Müllerian mimicry. It is named after Fritz Müller, a German zoologist. Müllerian mimicry occurs when animals from different species look alike and are either poisonous or bad tasting. Generally these animals are brightly colored. The colors are a warning sign to predators that the animals should be left alone.

Monarch and viceroy butterflies are good examples of Müllerian mimicry. Their colors and the markings on their wings look alike. The monarch is poisonous and the viceroy tastes very bad. A bird that has tried either one will likely stay away from both.

The bad-tasting viceroy, shown here, mimics the poisonous monarch. Birds that have tasted one butterfly with this coloring are unlikely to try another one.

A Closer Look at Müllerian Mimicry

Another good example of Müllerian mimicry is the poison dart frog, in South America and Central America, and the Mantella frog, from Madagascar. The bright colors of both species warn predators of their toxic, or poisonous, skin. The frogs are small but highly poisonous. Their enemies generally stay far away from them and any other frogs with bright colors.

The **indigenous** people who live in the rain forest sometimes use the frog's **toxin** when they go hunting. They rub the tips of their arrows or darts on the skin of one or two frogs. This is why the frogs are known as poison dart or poison arrow frogs.

Though not all poison dart frogs look alike, they all have brightly colored skin. These bright colors let predators know the animal is poisonous.

Crazy Copycat Facts!

1. Mimicry happens in both plants and animals.

2. Certain ant-eating spiders mimic ants and this makes it easier for them to enter an ant colony.

3. Some birds, such as parrots and mockingbirds, mimic other bird's songs and sometimes other sounds, such as car alarms or voices.

4. Most mimics are insects, such as butterflies and moths, but mimicry also appears in spiders, snakes, frogs, fish, and other animals.

5. Chances of staying safe from predators increase when there are more models than mimics in a group.

6. Hoverflies, which look like honeybees, even make a sound like a bee makes when predators are near.

7. A few rhymes have been made up to help people tell the difference between coral snakes and their mimics. One example is, "If red touches yellow, avoid this fellow."

8. Hawk-moth caterpillars tuck in their heads, bend their bodies, show off their eyespots, and mimic snakes. They even wiggle from side to side to look more like a snake!

What Is Self-Mimicry?

Have you ever looked at a caterpillar and wondered which end was its head? Some animals have a type of defense called self-mimicry. These creatures often have body parts that mimic other parts of their own bodies. Some of these animals have markings called eyespots.

Self-mimicry is not used only by prey. Sometimes predators, such as frogmouth catfish, use self-mimicry, too. A frogmouth catfish has something on its tongue that looks like food other fish like to eat. The catfish lies very still, sticking out its long tongue. When a small fish approaches the "food," the catfish quickly eats the fish!

This longlure frogfish hides itself among sponges and moves a body part that looks like food. When a fish swims over for lunch, it gets eaten instead!

More About Eyespots

Some species of butterflies, moths, fish, frogs, and caterpillars have large circles on their bodies. These circles are called eyespots because they look like eyes.

Predators generally like to approach their prey without being seen. Eyespots confuse predators and they come toward their prey from the wrong side. The prey sees them coming and has time to escape.

Eyespots can keep animals safe in another way, too. Some animals, such as Io moths, hawk-moth caterpillars, and false-eyed frogs, have markings that look like the eyes of a big animal. These "eyes" scare away predators.

The owl butterfly gets its name from the large eyespots on its wings, which look like the eyes of an owl.

More About Body-Part Mimics

Let's take a closer look at the animals that mimic another body part. This form of mimicry helps animals draw attention away from important body parts, such as the head. Predators will likely bite a part of the body that will not hurt the prey as much.

There are some snakes that have tails that look like their heads or heads that look like their tails. This mimicry saves the snake because a bird trying to eat the snake might not bite the head. The bird could also miss catching the snake if it starts moving in the opposite direction from what the bird expected.

Can you tell which end is the head on this caterpillar? With luck, a bird will not be able to spot the head easily either!

Why Is Mimicry Important?

Mimicry helps an animal live longer in its habitat, which is the goal of most animals. Over time, animals that looked like something that scared off or confused predators lived. The animals that did not have these special colors or markings did not.

At the same time, the predators have adapted, too. They have learned which animals might hurt them and they stay away from those animals. Changing when the environment changes is key to a species' survival over time. Mimicry is just one of the many tools animals have adapted to live in our ever-changing natural world!

Glossary

adapted (uh-DAPT-ed) Changed to fit requirements.

dangerous (DAYN-jeh-rus) Might cause hurt.

defenses (dih-FENT-ez) Things a living thing has or does that help keep it safe.

environment (en-VY-ern-ment) All the living things and conditions of a place.

indigenous (in-DIH-jeh-nus) Having started in and coming naturally from a certain place.

mimics (MIH-miks) Things that copy something else closely.

poisons (POY-zunz) Things that cause pain or death.

predators (PREH-duh-terz) Animals that kill other animals for food.

prey (PRAY) An animal that is hunted by another animal for food.

scales (SKAYLZ) The thin, dry pieces of skin that form the outer covering of snakes, lizards, and other reptiles.

species (SPEE-sheez) One kind of living thing. All people are one species.

toxin (TOK-sun) A type of poison.

Index

Web Sites

Due to the changing nature of Internet links, PowerKids Press has developed an online list of Web sites related to the subject of this book. This site is updated regularly. Please use this link to access the list:

www.powerkidslinks.com/cnature/mimic/